101 Ways to Simplify Your Life

Laura Aridgides, Ph.D.

ISBN: 1461125774
EAN-13: 978-1461125778

© 2012 First Edition
© 2014 Second Edition
Laura Aridgides and OrganizeNOW, LLC.
All rights reserved.

This work may not be translated or copied in whole or in part without the written permission of the author except for brief excerpts in connection with reviews or scholarly analysis. Use in connection with any form of information storage and retrieval, electronic adaptation, computer software, or by similar or dissimilar methodology now known or hereafter developed is forbidden. The use in this publication of trade names, trademarks, service marks, and similar terms, even if they are not identified as such, is not to be taken as an expression of opinion as to whether or not they are subject to proprietary rights.

This book is dedicated to everyone who needs a little more simplicity in the chaos of everyday life.

"For I know the plans I have for you," declares the Lord, "plans to prosper you and not to harm you, plans to give you a hope and a future."
Jeremiah 29:11 - NIV

Why This Book?

In the past year, I have been on a journey... a journey of simplification. Along the way, I have blogged about my experience (at www.ThisMessyHome.com) and many have asked me about my journey.

I am, by no means, finished with the journey to simplifying my life, but there are many things that I have done that have helped me to simplify. And that, my friends, is why I am writing this book. It is to equip you, empower you and inspire to you simplify your life. To do less and have more.

When you take time to simplify your life, the rewards are endless. As a starting point, I challenge you to find just three things to incorporate into your life from this book. Enjoy the journey!

To your success,
Dr. Laura Aridgides
November 2012

Acknowledgements

Thank you!

To you the reader. Thank you for selecting this book to enjoy! I hope reading this book will encourage, inspire, and equip you to take charge and discover the true treasure of simplifying your life and home.

To my parents who always encouraged me to reach for the stars.

To my family for their loving support.

To all of my direct sales friends. My life is better having known you. I thank you for 15+ years of wonderful memories. My prayer is that these pages will help you take your business to a new level.

What To Expect From This Book

The idea behind this book is to give you 101 different ways to simplify your life. Throughout the next 101 pages, you will see each page has a different tip, technique or strategy.

These may be read in any order, and they are also listed in no particular order.

Some ideas come with concrete action plans that you can put into place today to help simplify your life.

Other ideas are more abstract and may take longer to incorporate into your life.

Ready?

Let's dive in...

1. Make a Goal

I am a big believer in goal setting now. However, until I started my own business in 1999, I really didn't set goals. Then I discovered the world of being self-employed and learned that in order to achieve success, it was helpful to set goals!

Without goals, you are just riding along to an unknown destination. When there is no goal, how do you know when you have reached it? Now I set goals in every area of my life - both in business and personally.

My suggestion for you is to set a simplification goal as well. That could be trying one new idea from this book each week. Or it could be to eliminate one item from your home every day (like I did in the 75 in 75 Challenge). Your goal should be specific and trackable - some of my best achievements involved goals that were tracked along the way.

What will your simplification goal be?

2. Focus on What You Can Change

One thing that you must realize at the beginning is that not everyone will share your same viewpoint. This is unfortunate, because I believe that everyone can benefit from simplification, however, some will not embrace this area of life.

What can you do? The best thing is to focus on areas that you can change. For example, when I was decluttering my bedroom for the Minimalist Monday Mission, I focused on areas that were mine - my nightstand, my drawer in the vanity, my clothes - and I left the rest alone.

You may have a situation where your significant other or spouse is not as excited about simplifying as you. That is okay. Just focus on what you control, and what you can change. Leave the rest alone. And, in the end your example may just inspire those around you. I never did get my husband's nightstand decluttered, but he did go through his clothes!

Focus on what you can control and change and leave the rest for now.

3. Just Do Something

"A journey of a thousand miles begins with a single step" - Confucius

Do not get overwhelmed by all that there is to do each day. Do not get overwhelmed by the many things that you can do to simplify.
Just do something.

Just throw out one thing that is lying around. Just donate one shirt. Just cut up one credit card. Just eliminate one obligation from your calendar. Just be still for a minute. Just enjoy a luxurious soak in the tub. Just call your mother. Just declutter one area. Just simplify one task.

Just do something.

4. Live Simply

"Live simply so that others may simply live" - Gandhi

Look around you. We live in a world of chaos. But, you can choose another path...a life of simplicity.

What does living simply mean to you? Each person will have a different answer. For me, it means that I am living in a home that is peaceful. It is uncluttered and for those who live here, has become a haven of rest. Living simply for me also means that I choose to opt-out. Opt-out of over commitment, of watching lots of TV, of getting the latest greatest technology the moment it comes out, of consumerism, of overspending. And instead, choosing to live my life focusing on what matters most to me: my spiritual life, my family, and my friends. It means saying "no" to the unimportant to be able to say "yes" to the important.

How will you choose to live simply?

5. Become More Minimalist

Minimalism ties directly in to living simply. The fact is that clutter drains us - emotionally, physically, and mentally. When we choose to opt-out a natural byproduct for many is to become more minimalist.

My journey to minimalism began when I started decluttering my home in the 75 in 75 Challenge, and is still ongoing today. I have not gotten down to only owning 100 things, nor have I tried. I live in a modest home, and drive a car.

When people hear of minimalists, the first thing that they think of are those people who chose to live with 50 things, who are renting a small apartment, and who take public transportation and walk everywhere because they do not own a car. Although there are several people that I personally know that fit into this "minimalist mold", there are many more who do not.

To become more minimalist, you must rid yourself of the clutter, the excess that is holding you back from focusing on the most important things in your life. What is holding you back?

6. Declutter Your Home

Decluttering your home is one of the easiest, yet most powerful things that you can do to simplify your life. Remember that excess "stuff" wears us down. But, when you declutter your home, and remove the excess, you are left with those things that are important to you and your space.

Start with eliminating one item a day. What started out as a challenge to eliminate 75 items in 75 days for me, turned into eliminating 1,150 items from my home in 75 days. The result was nothing short of amazing!

First, I could not believe that I had so much in my home, and what is interesting is that I could not see a huge difference until I hit about 750 items removed from my home. And that was just the tip of the iceberg. I looked around and wondered where I had gotten all of this "stuff". The more and more I eliminated, the more I was spurred on to eliminate. It was sheer bliss!

Start now and eliminate one item a day!

7. 15 Minutes a Day

One of the biggest excuses I hear as I am coaching others is..."I don't have enough time". Yes, you do.

All you need is 15 minutes a day.

Start by thinking of the area in your home or life that is bothering you the most, and that is where you can spend your 15 minutes. Perhaps that is decluttering an area of your home, or perhaps it is spent reading, writing, or taking a walk.

15 minutes may not sound like a lot of time, but it adds up quickly. If you spend 15 minutes a day doing something important, by the end of the week, you will have spent over one hour doing something important. And it keeps adding up.

What will you do for 15 minutes today?

8. Reduce Your Junk Mail

Unfortunately, junk mail has become part of life for most of us. There are two main ways to take control of the junk mail:

1. Stop it from coming to your home.
2. Eliminate it quickly if it does get to your home.

First, to stop junk mail, I recommend that you opt-out of everything that you can.

To opt-out of credit card offers, visit: www.optoutprescreen.com.

To opt-out of direct mail, visit: www.dmachoice.org.

And finally, you will need to call each catalog that you receive in the mail as you get it to request to be removed from their mailing lists.

Secondly, when you get your mail, get in the habit of opening it over the trash can or near your recycling bin. Open your mail and immediately trash or recycle anything that is junk. Be sure to shred credit card offers, or other information with your name and address.
I use catalogs and shredded paper as packing materials, but you can recycle those as well.

9. Cancel Your Home Phone

In today's age of technology, most people have a cell phone. However, most people also still have a home phone as well.

Ask yourself if your home phone is really necessary? Most cell phone plans offer unlimited long distance (at least during certain hours) and are adequate enough to serve as your primary phone.

Years ago, we disconnected our home phone line and we have never regretted it. Most people who wanted to reach us simply called our cell phone anyway, and we hardly ever got calls that were not telemarketing calls on our home phone line.

Now there are even more choices, with free options like Skype and Google Talk, so cancel the home phone line, save some money, and have one less thing to worry about.

10. Use Your Voicemail

Speaking of phones, most of us jump to answer the phone when it rings, regardless of what we might be in the middle of doing. This is not using technology wisely.

Instead, control your calls by using your voicemail. When you are in the middle of something (dinner, a project, a meeting, etc.) put your phone on vibrate, and only answer if it could be someone calling with an emergency (your babysitter calling, etc.). Otherwise, let voicemail do the work for you.

On your voicemail message, let people know that you will be checking your voicemail once a day (or twice a day), and that you will call them back as soon as possible. This lets people know that you will return their calls, but perhaps not immediately. (By the way, Tim Ferriss' book <u>*The Four Hour Workweek*</u> has some great voicemail scripts.)

Then, fight the urge to constantly check your voicemail. Do check your voicemail once or twice a day, and return calls when it is convenient for you.

11. Stop Checking Email

Email is another area where most people get sucked in to a huge time wasting vortex. We feel the need to check our email multiple times during the day. There is really two parts to simplifying email:

Schedule a time to check and respond to emails. Turn off email notifications.

First, schedule a time during the day to deal with your emails. If you have your email open all day, start with checking it three or four times a day (morning, noon, afternoon, evening). Pare it down from there. The goal would be to get down to checking your email once a day or even less.

When you are not checking email, keep your email browser or program closed. This reduces the urge to see if you have any messages. Checking email frequently distracts us from keeping focus on the task we are doing, and ultimately wastes a lot of time. You can process your emails quicker when you do it in one big batch.

Second, turn off your email notifications. Always. Then you won't be reminded of new messages and get the urge to check your email again!

12. Use a Timer

Many people tell me that they wish they could just get more done. I have found that one of the things you can do to focus your time and energy on one project is to set a timer for a specific amount of time.

You know the saying... "How do you eat an elephant? One bite at a time."

That is the same way that you can tackle larger projects. Set a timer for 15 minutes and see how much you can accomplish in that time. Don't get distracted with other things; focus only on your current task at hand for the entire time.

It's really amazing what 15 minutes a day can do. If you declutter your home for 15 minutes a day, at the end of the week, you will have spent almost 2 hours decluttering! Do that for a month and you've spent almost an entire day decluttering!

Do you want to write or create? Spend 15 minutes a day. Read a good book? Spend 15 minutes a day. Get more organized? Spend 15 minutes a day.

Set your timer and GO!

13. Use Social Media The Smart Way

Let's face it...social media is here to stay. And, social media can be beneficial if used the right way...the smart way. But, you can also spend hours on Facebook and Twitter if you are not careful.

First, limit the number of friends (on Facebook) or people you follow (on Twitter) to meaningful relationships. You don't need to be friends with everyone on Facebook just because you can be. And you don't need to follow thousands of people on Twitter either. No one has time to read the umpteen million updates from your "friends".

Second, limit your time on Facebook and Twitter (as well as other sites). Set a timer (see #12) and choose to spend 15 minutes on Facebook or Twitter. Log in, check some of your friend's statuses or tweets, update your status or send a few tweets, and log off.

Third, if you have a business, create a business Facebook page, rather than a personal page. That way people can "like" your business and follow your updates, but you don't need to see theirs.

Think about your social media accounts...do you need to purge a few "friends"?

14. Focus on a Core Group of People

It's been said that humans can only tolerate around 150 connections. Anything more and you lose the quality of the relationship. However, it's also been said that each person knows about 2,000 people or acquaintances.

In today's age of high-tech social media connections galore, we have forgotten about the meaningful 150 and instead focused on the trivial 2,000.

To simplify, turn that around and focus on creating meaningful relationships with a core group of people. I would suggest that this group be no more than 150 people.

Think of family members, friends, mentors, and colleagues. Who is important to you and why? Who adds value to your life? Who challenges and inspires you? Who is there to lend an ear?

It's not that you shouldn't associate with the 2,000 acquaintances...you can...but at the same time, 95% of your focus should be on building and strengthening the relationships in your core group of 150.

15. Group Errands Together

Here's a practical tip for you. I'm always looking for ways to group errands together to save time. Rather than running out to the store multiple times during the week, unless it's an emergency, save your errands for a once-a-week outing.

I usually run errands on Fridays, as that's what I have found works best for me, but whatever works for you is fine. As I go through the week, and I think of something that needs to be done, I just add it to my list of errands. I also have an area in my home where I can group together items for my errand list (i.e.: dry cleaning, items to return, grocery list and coupons, bank deposits, items for the post office, etc.).

Grouping errands together is not only easier and simpler, but it also saves you time, and gas (which saves you money).

If you are used to running out to the stores multiple times a week, it will take you a few weeks to get used to not hopping in the car as soon as you think of something, but stick with it! It's so much easier!

16. Create Infinite Time

Infinite time is a concept that was first introduced to me by one of my coaches, Eric Lofholm. Although this concept very easily applies to the business world, it can also apply to your personal life as well.

The idea behind infinite time is to view time as an investment. When you invest 1 hour of your time in watching TV, what do you get back? The answer is nothing. When you invest 1 hour of time in spending time with your family, what do you get back? Well, you get back both the hour of activity with your family, plus the residual effects that spending time with your family can have (improved relationships, etc.). Now, when you invest 1 hour of time in self-improvement, what do you get back? You get the knowledge and skills to last you a lifetime, which is more than your 1 hour of time.

In the business world, this is easy to see. If I invest 1 hour in creating a video training lesson that I then offer for sale, what do I get back? Well, that investment of time never needs to be made again, but hypothetically, people could purchase that video training lesson indefinitely. Therefore, I created infinite time. It's all about getting the best return of investment for your time.

How could you apply this concept in your life right now?

17. Use a Schedule

Did you know that for every 15 minutes you spend planning, you could save an hour of time?

Take 15 minutes every Sunday evening and look at your schedule for the upcoming week. What do you have planned? Where are pockets of time that you could work on a project or other "to do" task? What do you need to do this week for business? What do you need to do this week with your family? What do you need to do this week for yourself?

Some people function best on a rigorous daily schedule, while others get by with a quick overview for the week. Find out what works best for you, but make time in your week to schedule your week.

And remember when you are making your schedule that people always underestimate the amount of time something will take, and overestimate how much they can do. So, allow for plenty of wiggle room in your schedule and breaks in between appointments or activities.

Make a commitment to start scheduling today!

18. The Daily "To Do" List

There is a right and a wrong way to do a "to do" list. Unfortunately, most people write down everything they could possibly think of and end up with a list a mile long. It's unrealistic to think that you can do so much, and it's also stressful having that huge list hanging over your head every day. There is a better way.

First, it IS important to create your "master to do list" and do a brain dump of everything you can remember that you need to do. Get all those tasks out of your head and on to paper or an online task list. But, then you must do the next step.

Use your master "to do" list to create a daily "to do" list. Your daily "to do" list should have no more than 10 items listed. Ever. Go through your master "to do" list and pick out the top 10 tasks. These are tasks that will provide you with value, or that have a deadline, etc. But, you are only allowed to pick 10.

Then we are going to narrow it down even more on step #19 next...

19. Implement the 80/20 Rule

Many of you have heard of the 80/20 Rule or Pareto's principal. In a nutshell: 80% of the effort will result in 20% of the results, and 20% of the effort will result in 80% of the results.

What does this mean? You can apply the 80/20 rule to many things in life...including your daily "to do" list.

So, when you look at your list of 10 tasks, 2 of the tasks, when completed will give you an impact or value equal to the other 8 tasks combined. These top 2 tasks are the ones you want to focus on at the start of each day.

When you start your day by working on the 2 things that are the most important for you to do, and that will give you the biggest impact, you will find that you are always getting more results and faster. Don't be tempted to go on to the other 8 tasks until you have worked as much as you can on those top 2 tasks.

What are your top 2 tasks for today?

20. The 2 Minute Rule

I love the 2 Minute Rule and it's totally revolutionized the way I do things around the house. Here's how it works:

If you have a task that can be completed in less than 2 minutes, do it right away.

This means that if you get a postcard in the mail reminding you that you need to schedule a visit to your dentist, since it takes less than 2 minutes to make that appointment, you are going to stop and do it right away. Then, you'll note the appointment in your calendar and throw the postcard out.

Unfortunately, what happens for many people is that they will see the postcard and think to themselves, "I'll just do that later", and then the postcard gets put in a pile. Then the next thing they come across gets added to that pile and before you know it, there is a mountain of things to do - almost all of which could have been handled in under 2 minutes right away!

Do you have a pile of things like that? Go through it today and start doing all those 2 minute tasks. Then commit to using the 2 minute rule from now on!

21. The 45 Minute Rule

The 45 minute rule is an absolute must for any large project or task. It's probably the sole reason I was able to work on my doctoral dissertation for 14 hours a day for many, many days.

Whenever you have a larger project or block of time that you will be working, it's important to take breaks every 45 minutes...hence the 45 minute rule. For every hour of time, you will work 45 minutes and take a 15 minute break.

When you are working for the 45 minutes, make sure to focus only on the task you are doing. Ignore everything else, and if possible, work in an area that has no distractions.

What to do on your 15 minute break is totally up to you. When I was doing my dissertation, I did a crosstitch project. You can get up, stretch, walk around, get a cup of water, or whatever! Just take a break.

Then, come back and focus again for another 45 minutes. Repeat this cycle until your time working is finished or your project is completed.

22. Create a Routine

Have you ever heard that children thrive on routine? This is true, but it's also true that **adults** thrive on routine too! So, simplify your days by creating routines wherever possible.

Do you have a series of things you do each morning? Create a routine. Perhaps you get up, take a shower, get dressed, eat breakfast and pray. Make that your morning routine.

How about creating routines at work? At noon, I have a routine that includes checking and responding to email, and checking and responding to voicemail, and then making phone calls.

When you create routines, you are creating familiarity. You are also creating habits. When something becomes a habit, you don't even have to think about it - you just do it.

I had small routines at different times during the day that create a larger "routine" day. This simplifies my days and helps me flow from one activity to the next.

23. Disconnect

We are surrounded by so much noise in our day-to-day lives: advertisements, cell phones, text messages, instant messages, Facebook, Twitter, and the list goes on.

While many of these things can be tools if used properly (cell phone, text messages, Facebook, Twitter), most of the noise we deal with is just that...noise.

Take time to disconnect.

Take an afternoon off, or a day off, and disconnect from the Internet, TV, and other distractions.

Go for a walk, read a good book, connect with your family, or spend time in nature.

I know several people who take "digital sabbaticals" weekly so they can step back, take a break from the chaos and rejuvenate. The times that I have done this were so refreshing, that I strive for a regular "digital sabbatical" every week.

24. Take a Walk

There is something magical about connecting with nature and going for a walk. Just a simple walk around the block or in your neighborhood does wonders for your soul (not to mention the exercise).

I find that taking a walk clears the mind, and I do some of my best thinking while walking. I just let my mind wander (if alone), or I can engage in great conversation (if I am walking with a friend).

As I mentioned in #23, with today's world so focused on the high-tech aspects, it's nice to take a break and return to the simpler things in life like taking a walk.

You'll feel rejuvenated and refreshed, and I challenge you (if weather permits) to make walking a regular part of your simplification routine.

25. Go to the Park

Here's another concept to help you return to simpler times. Go to the park.

Especially if you have children.

Take a family outing and go to the park. Play on the swings, and remember back to your childhood days as the wind blows through your hair.

Bring a soccer ball and kick it around together, or play a game of catch with a baseball and mitt.

While you are there, look at all of the beauty around you - allow your senses to fully expand and enjoy your surroundings. Notice the leaves as they wave in the breeze, or take time to watch the clouds drifting by.

Go to the park today.

26. Spend Time with Your Spouse

If you are married, your relationship with your spouse is the most important human relationship you can have. Take time to nurture this relationship by spending quality time with your spouse.

Set a regular "date night" with your spouse. It doesn't matter what you do or where you go - just be with each other. Talk to each other. Share dreams with each other.

If money is tight, have a "date night" at your home after the children go to bed. Cook a special meal, set the table for a romantic dinner for two, light the candles and enjoy each other's company. Sit up late and just talk.

When we are so busy that other things push their way to the top of our list, our relationship with our spouse suffers. Make it the priority that it deserves to be, and bless your relationship by spending time with each other regularly.

What will you do with your spouse this week?

27. Cook Dinner

It seems like the days of a nice home-cooked meal are few and far between. This is unfortunate, because there are so many benefits to a good home-cooked meal.

When you cook dinner, it usually means that you are home. So, when you have cooked your meal, be sure to sit the entire family down for dinner around the table. The family dinner table is another tradition that has fallen by the wayside, and desperately needs to be resurrected.

Spending time with your family around the table is one of the best things you can do for your family. The family dinner table is a time of sharing stories and experiences, and bonding together as a family unit. When you are at a restaurant you are competing with the noise around you. Instead, eat in today and focus on your family.

It doesn't have to be elaborate. Start by setting a "dinner time" so that your family knows when dinner will be served, and create the expectation that all family members need to be present at that time.

What will you cook for dinner tonight?

28. Eat Real Food

While you are cooking at home, you also have the ability to make better choices.

Choose to cook "real food".

You know what I mean - replace the processed junk that lines the grocery store shelves with food that is fresh, local (if possible) and in season. Your body will thank you for it.

When you eat better, you feel better, you function better, you sleep better, and you live better.

Perhaps you remember the saying, "Garbage in, garbage out". It's true. I know this from experience (sadly). I can tell you that eating "real food" is not only better for my body, but it's also simpler too.

It doesn't take me any more time to make something from scratch than it does to break out a box of processed food and nuke it in the microwave. There are great meals that you can make in no time at all. And, I feel great knowing that I am giving my body, and my family the best nutrition possible.

29. Exercise

Exercise is a simple thing that can also have a great impact. When you exercise, you feel rejuvenated!

I love to keep exercise simple. There is no need for big equipment or a gym membership. Just grab your walking shoes and go for a walk (see #24). Grab your soccer ball and head to the park with your children (see #25).

Or you can choose to do some simple exercises at home. Sit-ups, push-ups, lunges, and more - there are many effective exercises that you can do using your own body weight and no special equipment.

Just get up and get moving!

And, when you exercise, you'll find that you sleep better. I don't know about you, but when I get a great night's sleep (see #56), I always have a better day.

30. Clear Your Desk

Do you have a desk that you work from (either at home, or an outside workplace)?

Imagine this...you walk into your office and see your desk piled full of paper and sticky notes. You look at your desk and immediately a feeling of dread surfaces. You don't even want to sit down, much less get to work! A messy desk is not only stressful, but it's also very unproductive as well.

Instead, take time to make sure that when you leave your space every day, that the desktop area is kept clear. Then when you arrive the next day to work, you will be greeted by a nice clear space. It's calming to see a clear desk, and you'll even **want** to get to work!

If your desk is cluttered, spend 15 minutes today getting the space clear. If it's really bad, just dump everything into a big plastic container and then make a plan to go through that plastic container later. That way, you can start with a fresh surface.

How is your desk looking?

31. Get in the Zone

While you are working on your desktop area (see #30), it helps to use the zone concept.

Think of your desk as a bulls eye. When you sit at your chair, you are at the center of the bulls eye. Everything you can touch from your seat is in your "red zone". The red zone should only contain items that you use on a daily basis (or several times a week). Within the red zone, your actual desktop is the most important space and is considered "prime real estate". Make sure you watch what you put on your desk. Less is best, and if something can be easily stored in a drawer to enable your desktop space to remain clear, that's the best option.

The next ring out from your bulls eye is the "yellow zone". The yellow zone is when you must get out of your chair and walk a few steps to reach the items in this zone. These items will be things that you use several times a month at least.

Lastly, there is the "green zone" which is everything else that you only use a few times a year or even less. Those items are stored out of the area (i.e., across the room on a bookshelf, or downstairs in a storage closet)

Spend time today to get your zones in order! You'll be able to function better!

32. Make a Declutter Schedule

I firmly believe that everyone should declutter his or her home at least once every few years. If it's been a while for you, or you've never decluttered your home since you moved in 10 years ago, then it's time to schedule a decluttering session.

Most homes cannot be decluttered in a weekend, or even a month of weekends. Realistically, we have other obligations from work and family that bid for our time as well.

So, I recommend that you create a decluttering schedule. Decide on a time frame for your decluttering project. For my Minimalist Monday Mission: Declutter 365, I decided to declutter my home over the course of a year.

Decide on what areas to declutter first (I usually like to start with areas that are bothering me the most). Then, find someone to hold you accountable. For me, it's blogging about the week's results with before and after pictures that hold me accountable, but it could be a friend or family member that will help keep you on track.

Challenge: Make your decluttering schedule this week.

33. The Most Important Question

As you move through each day, it's very easy to get off track. But, I have found getting back "on track" is as easy as one simple question.

What is the most important question?

Create a habit of asking yourself this one question throughout the day:

"Is this the best use of my time?"

If the answer is yes, then great! Keep doing what you are doing!

But, if the answer is no, then shift gears and do something that is a better use of your time.

34. Use a Planner

I firmly believe that for most people, you need to write down what you want to accomplish. I've even heard the saying, "What doesn't get scheduled, doesn't get done."

But, in order to keep track of life and our obligations, you must have somewhere to record these thoughts, appointments, tasks, etc.

Enter...the planner.

This is one of my most essential tools and I carry it with me everywhere. A planner can be digital (on a smartphone) or paper (Franklin Covey has a great selection of paper planners), depending on your personal preference. But, above all, you must do two essential things:

1. Carry your planner with you everywhere.
2. Write everything down!

A planner is only helpful if it is used; so decide on what kind of planner you like, and start using one today!

35. Read

When was the last time you curled up with a good book, just for pleasure?

While I am a BIG advocate of reading for improvement (and I recommend that you regularly read self-improvement types of books), I also think there is a place for losing yourself in a nice fictional story.

Why not make it part of your daily routine? If reading for pleasure, I suggest reading before you go to bed - just 15 or 30 minutes is great. If reading for improvement, I suggest reading first thing in the morning - again, 15 or 30 minutes.

Grab a cup of coffee or tea, and carve out a few minutes of reading each day.

36. Relax

Relaxation is part of rejuvenating you! Think about what relaxes you. For each person, this may be different. I, for one, enjoy massages or sitting on a beach or basking in the sun for relaxation, but I also enjoy reading, crosstitching and quilting for relaxation too.

The first step in relaxation is to find something that you enjoy doing, or just do nothing at all.

The second step in relaxation is to schedule your time of relaxation! In today's high-paced society, you may find that unless you schedule your time to relax, it will not happen.

Make time to relax and recharge! You'll be able to accomplish more in the long run!

What will you do this week to relax?

37. Quiet Time

I have found that my days always go better when I make time in the morning for quiet time. As a Christian, I choose to use that time to read the Bible, pray, and talk to God.

It is this quiet time in the morning that prepares me for the day ahead. When I miss it, I can tell, and the day does not go as smoothly.

What can you do for a quiet time? Will you pray? Meditate? Read God's Word? Spend time in nature? Enjoy a cup of coffee on your porch watching the sunrise?

Plan a quiet time each day...start today!

38. Emotional Detachment

There are times, especially in work situations, where our emotions get in the way and wreak havoc. While it is good to remain emotionally attached to the outcomes of many situations, there are some situations where it is best to choose emotional detachment.

For example, part of my business is calling potential clients. I used to get emotionally attached to the outcome - whether they said yes or no to what I had to offer. This in turn caused problems with self-esteem (if they say "no" to what I have to offer, they are saying "no" to me...of course...this is not true at all, but it's how our brains think!).

Instead, if I can let go of the outcome, and just focus on the process of asking, then what they say in response doesn't matter to me. A "no" becomes just as good of an outcome as a "yes". This is because I can separate my personal emotions from the situation and know that when a potential client says "no" to what I am offering, it is not personal, it's just a "no". And then a "no" becomes no big deal!

Let go of the outcome and practice selective emotional detachment.

Where could this technique help you?

39. Use Google

Okay, I admit it, I am a recent Google complete convert and I had no idea the depth of what I was missing!

Although I have used Google mail for my email for a long time, I did not take the time to explore many of the amazing features that everyone with a gmail account has access to. Many of these features have simplified my routine on a daily basis, and helped me consolidate things into one place, plus there are many fantastic things yet to explore!

Here are just a few of Google's features that I have used so far that I love:

1. Google Documents - Store documents online - this is how I have transferred many of my files to "the cloud" making them accessible from anywhere and any computer with Internet access. I love how it saves your work automatically too!

2. Picasa Web Photos - Store photos online - I store all of my photos for my blog here, and can share with friends and family quickly and easily. I can edit my photos in Picnik, which is part of Picasa.

3. Google Calendar - I use this as my main planner (see #34), and in syncs automatically with my iPod/iPhone.

4. Google Contacts - I have all of my contacts listed here, which also syncs to my iPod/iPhone and I keep notes on potential clients here too.

5. Web Stuff - I use Google Analytics and Feedburner to handle my web statistics.

Where could you use Google to help simplify your personal or business life?

40. Get Rid of One Item a Day

So many people look at where I am today on my minimalist journey (still in the middle, but I have eliminated over 3,000 items from my home at the time of this writing), and they are overwhelmed. They ask me, "Where do I start?"

My answer is always the same.

Start by getting rid of one item a day from your home.

That's how I started, and one thing leads to the next, and to the next, and before you know it, you've started to make an impact on the things around you and your space looks clearer, it becomes more inviting, peaceful and relaxing. And it all starts with one item.

Look around and I bet you will be able to easily find something to eliminate today. You can recycle it, donate it, throw it out or sell it. It doesn't matter how it gets out of your home, just that it does!

Tomorrow, repeat the process! And again the next day too! Make a game of it (that's what I did), and see where it takes you.

What will you eliminate today?

41. Unsubscribe

Do you ever get an email and wonder how on earth you possibly got on that person's mailing list? What about an unwanted mailing or catalog? I mentioned how to reduce your junk mail (see #8), and the same concept applies to email as well.

Unsubscribe.

Unsubscribe.

Unsubscribe.

If you get an email that is not **essential** to your daily life, take a few seconds to hit the unsubscribe button on the bottom of the email and declare your freedom!

After I ruthlessly unsubscribed from most of my emails, I noticed an immediate difference in the amount of email I received every day. It was cut in half! But, beware, you must be on guard and do not let your defenses down. Be careful in giving out your email address and if you notice unwanted emails popping up, unsubscribe immediately!

42. Turn Off the Phone

We are connected (it seems) for every waking moment of the day. Sometimes, however, it is good to disconnect (see #23). An easy way to disconnect is simply to turn off the phone (this means cell phones too!).

Being available 24/7 is both a blessing in many ways, and also a hindrance.

Remember the times before cell phones? We survived not being connected all the time, and you can still survive today without being connected all day too!

Turn off the phone when you are in places where a phone call would be an interruption, such as a movie, a meeting, or even your family dinner (see #27).

Or turn off your phone for a time of rest, a nap (see #100) or relaxation (see #36).

You will find that the world will still be waiting when you turn it back on :)

43. Go Digital

When 95% of the paper that we file will never be referenced again, look for other ways to store essential files. And in today's world, that often means storing them digitally.

The first step, of course, is to purge anything that is not absolutely necessary. File what you need paper copies of for legal reasons, etc. and the rest...digitize.

I personally use the Neat scanner to scan in page after page of documents. The scanner works fine, but the magic is in the software behind the scanner, which allows amazing search capabilities.

What do I send to "the cloud" for storage?

Cards, photos, receipts, papers, documents for business, business cards, and just about anything I can!

Then I put the files into my free Dropbox account so I can access them from any computer.

Finally, shred or trash everything you have scanned! Ah...digital freedom!

44. Drink Water

With our bodies being made up mostly of water, it makes sense that we should drink more of it!

But alas...most do not...including me!

However, I have found some simple things that make a big difference in the amount of water I drink.

First, check the taste. I don't think water should have a taste! For me, with well water, our water is fantastic, but you might need a water filter if you are in the city to get rid of chlorine, etc. Or, consider adding a drop or two of lemon essential oil to your water!

Second, make it easy to access. I always drink more water when I have it right there with me. Since I don't like to drink from plastic water bottles (leeching, etc.) and metal water bottles give the water a metallic taste (in my opinion), I chose a Lifefactory glass water bottle, which is amazing! I carry it everywhere!

What will you do today to drink more water?

45. Just Say NO!

With so many things vying for our time each day, there is a limit to how much you can do. We cannot possibly say "yes" to everything, so there is always something we must say "no" to.

However, this process does not have to be a guilt-ridden one, but can instead be a very freeing process.

Everyone has priorities, and when you say "yes" to something, you are automatically saying "no" to something else. When you choose to spend your time wisely, and say "yes" to the things that are most important to you, the impact of what you choose to do will be greater than if you make unwise decisions on where to spend your time.

So, learn to say "no" to the unimportant, so you can say "yes" to the important. For example, I always say "no" to fund raising, chairperson requests, bake sales, etc. because those things do not bring me in direct contact with my child. But, I will gladly say "yes" to field trip chaperone or assisting in a class project, because those opportunities allow me to spend time with my child.

It's all about choices. What will you say "no" to today?

46. Stop Wearing Makeup

This suggestion may take some getting used to for you ladies reading, but trust me when I tell you that I love not wearing makeup!

I stopped wearing makeup at the end of my senior year in high school, and have not worn it again, except for my wedding, and the occasional lip-gloss or concealer, for the past 15+ years.

When you don't wear makeup, there are many simplification benefits. It takes less time to get ready in the morning, and less time in the evening too. There is less storage space needed for cosmetics and toiletries. It is easier to travel lightweight. And there is less cost overall - no need for makeup or the expensive cleansers to take it all off!

Plus, there is a benefit to having your skin be able to breathe as nature intended, and I find my complexion is as healthy now as when I was in high school.

Why don't you try not wearing makeup for a weekend? Then try a week? Although it takes time getting used to looking in the mirror and seeing something different then what you are used to, it's worth it!

47. Your Morning Routine

Remember when I said that creating a routine is a huge time saver (see #22)?

Let's focus on the morning routine, because I find that it sets the tone for the entire day.

Here's what my routine looks like:
1. Get up, stretch in bed, pray.
2. Shower, get dressed.
3. Make breakfast/lunches, take vitamins, drink water.
4. Take children to school.
5. Quiet time for 15-30 minutes.
6. Read for 15-30 minutes.
7. Review the daily "to do" list and schedule.
8. Begin working my tackling the most important project of the day.

Now think of your morning routine. What do you do that could be simplified? Eliminated? What should you add in?

Aim to start each day with the best possible routine you can!

48. Clean Out Your Closet

For the past 4 months (as of this writing), I have been **living with 33 pieces of clothing and accessories**. It's been a fun experience to participate in Courtney Carver's Project 333, and it's also made me realize that I have an abundance of clothes, and my guess would be that you do too.

Early on in the 75 in 75 Challenge, I cleaned out my closet and donated a bunch of stuff to Goodwill. It was easy to do this first round, because there were obvious things that were outdated, damaged, or that no longer fit, and it was easy to part with those things.

Then I moved on to Minimalist Monday Mission and cleaned out my closet again. I loaded up with another big bag of items for Goodwill, having lived three months since the previous closet cleaning; it was easy to see some more that had to go.

But, I still saw excess. So, for fun, I embarked on Project 333 with Courtney and many others, and saw my closet in a whole new light. After living (very comfortably) on 33 items (included shoes, jackets, accessories), I now have another bag full of items ready for Goodwill. And, I can tell you, without a doubt, less is more in your closet!

I challenge you to take the first step and go

through your closet. Try on everything and eliminate anything you do not love and feel fantastic in! Then do it again in 3 months!

49. Chose Classic Clothes

When you are cleaning out your closet, I would recommend that you stick with keeping clothes that are classics.

You know...the clothes that are in basic colors and patterns, and that never go out of style.

If your closet is mostly made up of classic clothes in a few different color combinations, it becomes very easy to coordinate your outfits and get dressed in the morning.

This helps simplify your entire morning routine, because you can easily mix and match clothes and know that you will get a winning combination.

Do not be afraid to invest a little more in good quality classic clothes that will last longer than some of the cheaper varieties. And, make sure that anything you purchase is something that makes you look great and feel great too!

Most of my closet is made up of classic clothes, and they have stood the test of time (and the decluttering and cleaning of the closet too)!

50. Be Present

If you are on vacation, be present 100% in that vacation.

If you are spending time with your family, be present 100% in your family.

If you are at work completing a project, be present 100% in that project.

We discount others and our experiences if we are anything less than 100% present in the moment. There is a time for work, and a time for play. There is a time for family, and a time to be alone.

When you are at work, but are thinking about something else, you are not giving 100% to your work. Likewise, when you are with your family, but you are thinking about what you need to do at work, you are not giving your family 100% either.

Be present. Be in the moment.
100% of the time.

51. Focus

I'm laughing at the irony of writing this page as I force myself to **focus** on the task at hand...finishing this book!

But, when you focus on one thing at a time, you tend to get that thing done faster.

Turn off your Internet, close your browser, turn of the TV, and focus on what needs to be done.

Start your day by focusing on the most important thing you need to do that day, and aim to keep your focus strong until the task is done.

There are so many distractions in everyday life that it's important to take a few breaths and ... focus!

52. Serve Others

When I am having a rough day, or thinking about my problems, there is always something that works every time to rid me of these negative feelings.

That something is to serve others.

Find a way to get the focus off of yourself and on to others. What can you do today that will be a blessing for your spouse, children, friend or stranger?

Could you do the dishes because you know they need to be done? How about make a special snack to greet your children as they come home from school? Or, is there an elderly person in your community that you could have over for dinner? What about a friend that may be having a hard time...could you take them out to coffee?

It's amazing how serving others will brighten your mood and give you true JOY (Jesus First, Others Next, Yourself Last)!

53. Be Optimistic

I must admit, in the interest of full disclosure, that optimism does not come naturally to me. I would say that I view the cup half empty more often than not.

But the good news is that you can make a difference in your mood by being optimistic on purpose.

To be optimistic for some comes naturally, and those of you in this category should consider yourselves blessed. For the rest of us, optimism can be learned.

And, as a benefit, people who are optimistic have better health than those who are not.

Plus, it's just more fun and exciting to view the glass half full. Next time you find yourself being pessimistic about something, try to turn it around and transfer your pessimism into optimism. It takes a conscious awareness to realize that you are being negative in the first place, but the more you practice turning it around, the easier it gets!

How can you be optimistic today?

54. Laugh

Want to reduce stress and feel better today?

Laugh!

You have no doubt heard the saying, "Laughter is the best medicine", but there is truth to that statement!

Laughter combats stress, relaxes your body, boosts the immune system and makes you feel great!

So, tell some funny jokes today, or go rent a funny movie and laugh!

55. Love Unconditionally

Unconditional love is the kind of love that knows no boundaries. It is not based on actions (or the lack thereof), but is instead a deep love that comes from the depths of our souls.

This is the love that God has for each of us. He loves us no matter what we have done.

It is so easy to withdraw love from someone who has hurt or upset us, and I know that I have been guilty of this in the past.

But, when we learn to love each other unconditionally, we choose to look past the faults and failures and love each other as we are.

Loving unconditionally releases us to see the good in others.

Who needs your unconditional love today (even though they may not deserve it)?

56. Get Enough Sleep

Most of us do not get enough sleep on a day-to-day basis, but did you know that if you are shortchanging yourself in the sleep arena, that you are creating a sleep debt?

Researchers at Stanford have found that when we do not get enough sleep (and this will vary from person to person, but it's commonly around the 8 hour range), we create a sleep debt, and that this sleep debt does not go away until we catch up by getting more sleep!

The solution?

Make sure that you get enough sleep each night and if you are still feeling drowsy, chances are you are still carrying around a sleep debt of your own. The more sleep debt you have, the harder it is to stay awake, no matter the time.

But, when we take time to get enough sleep each night, then in the morning, we awake feeling refreshed and ready to go!

And, if you can, why not sneak a quick 20 minute nap in here and there throughout your week. Studies show that a quick nap is refreshing, and it will help you make up your sleep debt.

57. Create Systems

In our day-to-day routine, we all tend to have things that we do that are repeated.

For example, in business, I am always calling prospects and following up with them. It's part of my day-to-day business routine, and in my home, I will always have to do laundry.

So, to simplify these regular tasks, we can create systems. A system is something that you do each time you encounter that task that helps you simplify and streamline the task.

In the work example, I have a checklist of steps I take for each prospect that includes calling, writing, emailing and follow up. I never wonder what comes next, because I know each person will go through the "system" that I use for prospecting.

In the home example, I have a system I use when doing laundry. Specifically, I do laundry all on one day (you may need to do multiple days each week depending on the size of your family), and I wash the clothes in the same order every time. When laundry is done, it is hung up for the owner to put away. It's the same every week.

Where can you create a system to help you streamline and simplify?

58. Find Your Keys

Create a specific place in your home near the entrance of your home for your keys and wallet and you will save yourself hours of searching for both.

In my home, we have a key hanger right as you walk through the door that holds our keys until we walk through the door again.

I also have a specific spot reserved for my purse, and my husband has a spot reserved for his wallet.

When we come through the door, we hang up the keys and put our purse/wallet in it's designated spot. That way, when we leave again, there is no searching. They are right where they are supposed to be.

You can take this concept and apply it to other commonly lost items as well, such as the TV remote.

Do you have a spot for your keys?

59. Breathe

We do it everyday, unconsciously, breathing in and out, in and out. It's a part of life.

But, when done intentionally, breathing can be relaxing and semi-meditative as well.

This especially works when you are emotional or angry, hence the "count to 10 before responding" solution for situations where you are upset.

The proper way to breathe is to breathe deeply, involving your diaphragm. Your stomach should expand and contract with your breath. Some find it helpful to count as you breathe in and out and focus on your breathing technique.

There are many benefits to breathing deeply, including reducing stress and anxiety, increasing oxygen in your cells and elevating your mood.

So, today, don't just breathe…really **breathe.**

60. Downsize

The more I eliminate, the more life gets easier.

Less "stuff" in my house means less cleaning, and less stress. And when you have less "stuff" you could even downsize your living arrangements saving you financially as well.

Deep down we all know that "stuff" doesn't buy happiness.

If you need confirmation of this, just look for a family that has very little. Most families, even despite difficult circumstances, have great joy with less.

There are many benefits to downsizing, eliminating, simplifying...

What will you do today to downsize?

61. Guard Your Time

Time is something we never get back. Once it passes, it cannot be changed.

Each day we are given 24 hours, and it is up to us what we do with those 24 hours.

No one has more time than another. We are all equal.

Imagine you were given $1,440 to spend one day. There was only one rule...you had to spend it before the day was over. At the end of the day, whatever you did not spend, you lost. The next day, you were given $1,440 to spend again.

It is the same with our time. We have 1,440 minutes each day to make an impact on the lives of others and leave a legacy for future generations.

Think about how you spent your time today? Do you have regrets? Should you have spent your time more wisely?

Guard your time, each and every day.

62. Life's Speed Bumps

Everyone has speed bumps that they will encounter on the road of life.

It's how you respond to these speed bumps that matters.

"What is the difference between an obstacle and an opportunity? Our attitude toward it. Every opportunity has a difficulty and every difficulty has an opportunity." -- J. Sidlow Baster

"Obstacles don't have to stop you. If you run into a wall, don't turn around and give up. Figure out how to climb it, go through it, or work around it." -- Michael Jordan

What are the speed bumps in your life? How can you turn these obstacles into opportunities?

63. Never Give Up

Perhaps you have heard the saying, "The only way to fail is to quit."

This is true in many areas of life.

If something is truly worth doing, then it is also worth fighting for. Never give up. Keep fighting until the finish.

In my career as a coach and an entrepreneur, I have seen this played out before me countless times. Often someone works hard toward a goal, runs into an obstacle (or two or three) and gives up. Many times they give up just shy of their goal.

In the heat of the moment, they cannot see what I can see, but I know that if they had just pushed through the obstacle, just kept their sights on the goal ahead, just kept doing something, that they would have reached it. But, instead, they failed, because they quit.

Never give up.

64. What Would You Take?

Imagine an emergency where all of your family was safe, but you had only one minute to gather what you wanted to save from your home, and everything else would be completely destroyed.

What would you take?

Would you take the wedding picture album, the computer, your important documents? The antique painting, the ring your mother wore?

Many things would be lost, and only a few saved. What you would save tells you what is important to you. When you view your belongings through this lens, there is a clear distinction between what brings you joy that you would try to save, or the other things that you would choose to leave behind.

So, do you really need everything you would leave behind? Make a plan today to release yourself from those unnecessary possessions.

65. The Envelope System

I am always looking for ways to simplify my finances and one of the easiest and quickest things you can do to simplify finances is to use Dave Ramsey's Envelope System.

In a nutshell, decide on what budget categories that you have that you can use cash to pay for items. We choose to pay cash for: groceries, medical bills, haircuts, miscellaneous, eating out, and blow money (you can use this for whatever you want). Then, once you have decided the categories and the amounts you will spend, simply withdraw that amount and place it in the corresponding envelope.

Throughout the month, spend money from the envelope, paying in cash for every transaction out of the corresponding envelope. When the money is gone, you are done for the month. This may mean that you need to get creative when you see that you only have $10 left for groceries for a week!

Paying in cash ensures that you are consciously spending, and you will often spend less when you pay in cash than via credit card, plus it's the simplest most effective system I have found for basic monthly transactions.

67. Your Audio/Video Collection

Simplifying your audio/video collection can be a monumental task, especially if your audios and videos are mixed media collections.

To start the simplification process, treat each collection separately. First, take all of your videos out to one central location. Collect them from throughout the house. Sort through and discard any broken or missing videos/cases. Next, group videos together according to type (VHS, DVD, Blue-Ray, etc.), and then sort through each collection to decide which ones you will keep. When you are deciding what to keep and what to eliminate, consider what the video is on (is it a VHS that is of poor quality?) and whether you will honestly ever watch it again. If there is any doubt, eliminate it.

The videos that you decide to keep should be stored neatly, in alphabetical order, in a storage case or bookshelf. All videos that you are eliminating can be sold, donated, or given away.

Repeat the process with the audios, and in both cases, keep in mind the move to more of a digital platform. Could you digitize your movies and then play them from your computer? What about converting your audios into MP3 files so you can store them on your computer and play them without the actual disk?

68. Photographs

Most homes have a multitude of pictures, both displayed on the walls and shelves, and also in photo albums or boxes.

To simplify your photographs, first ask yourself if those that you are currently displaying on your walls or shelves bring you great joy when you see them? If not, take them down (you can always put them in an album or scan them later). This will reduce the clutter on your walls and shelves, and will also highlight the photos you have left behind that mean something to you.

For other pictures and albums, gather all your photographs in one place. Sort through and throw out any pictures that are poor quality. Keep only the best of the best. Put those photos that you have kept in chronological order, and label events (use can use sticky notes for this) so that you won't forget.

If you are a scrapbooker, and enjoy doing it by hand, then plan quality time to work on your scrapbook project regularly. Or, you can try piecing your scrapbook together digitally – I have used Picaboo and love the service!

Once finished, display your books nicely, and remember to look through them regularly (otherwise, why make them?).

69. Clean Your Computer

Your computer is a digital filing cabinet, and needs to be treated that way. Your computer should have files stored within folders (and sub-folders when applicable), and it should be kept neat and clear.

Here are the steps I take when cleaning out my computer files:

1. Go through each document, delete what you don't need.
2. Rename any files you are keeping if needed, and move them into the correct file folder.
3. Backup all files on an external hard drive (I use Western Digital's Passport).
4. Covert any document you can to a Google document (see #39). After converting you can delete the file on your computer (but keep your backup on the external hard drive).
5. Put all of the other files into your Dropbox account (See #43).
6. Uninstall any programs you no longer need.
7. Run your anti-virus protection and anti-spyware protection.
8. Run your computer's disk defragmentation program.
9. Backup your entire computer on an external source (I use the Rebit drive).
10. Store your backup sources in a safe-deposit box, or fire safe.
11. Repeat every 6-12 months, and to keep your computer clear in the mean time, when you

download something be sure to save it to the correct folder.

If your computer needs a major overhaul, after the steps above, you can do a system reboot using the disc that came with your computer. This will wipe your hard drive clean and you will start fresh as though your computer just came out of the box.

If you choose to do this, make sure you have saved all files externally that you wish to keep, and that you have access to your program files to download (or on disc) so you can re-install the essential programs that you want to use.

I have found that starting from scratch does seem to fix most "slow" computer issues, and can be a useful tool if your computer is loaded with lots of unnecessary programs and files.

70. Books

If you love to read, then chances are you might have a nice sized book collection. I know, because I used to as well.

To simplify my books (and the amount of space needed to store them), here are a few suggestions:

First, if you have read a book, only keep it if it is life changing, or you absolutely positively will read it again, or it has some very significant sentimental value.

If you have read the book and it does not fit the above description, then list it for sale (Amazon or Paperback Swap are good choices), or donate it to the local library.

When purchasing a new book, first, check to see if it is available through your library. If not, consider purchasing the book digitally (although I have a Kindle, you can also download the Kindle app for free from Amazon, allowing you to read Kindle books right on your own computer) to save space (and trees).

And, if you must get a paper copy of the book, limit the number of books you have on hand that you have not read at any given moment, and vow to give/sell the book once you are done reading!

71. Scan It

Whenever you need to keep something, rather than keeping the original copy tucked away in a file folder taking up space somewhere, why not scan it instead?

Unless I need to keep something for legal reasons, I scan it.

I use my Neat scanner to scan bills, statements, receipts, cards, children's artwork, and much more!

By scanning something you are saving space in your home and work area. This leads to less clutter, especially paper clutter.

When items come in to my home that I want to scan, I just place them in a special folder in my filing cabinet designated for scanning. Then, once a week, I take the entire folder out and scan it all in to the computer.

Remember when you digitize things that are important to you, you must back up your data, and have multiple external backups that are safe too (in a fire safe or safety deposit box).

72. Don't Upgrade

In our consumerist society, companies count on you "keeping up with the Joneses" to keep them in business. Companies are constantly coming out with the latest and greatest things and gadgets.

But, resist the urge to be like the masses. Just because something comes out in a later version doesn't mean you need to toss your perfectly good one aside and go scramble out to buy the next version. And just because your neighbor or friend has something, doesn't mean that you have to have it too.

Don't get me wrong...I love technology and I am all for the cutting-edge technology that is here today, but I don't have the need to go get the latest thing if I either don't need it, or already have something similar in good working condition.

The pressure to constantly upgrade not only bankrupts our wallets, but it also overflows our landfills at the same time.

Break the cycle of consumerist spending and upgrades! And, when you do **need** something, do your research and buy a quality product that will last.

73. Cut It In Half

Go to your kitchen and find...**the drawer**...

You know the one I am talking about...the junk drawer!

We all have them! Now open yours up and make simplifying your junk drawer a game. See if you can cut the number of things in the drawer in half.

First, take everything out. Then, throw out anything broken or unusable. Now, as you pick up each item that remains ask yourself if that item is a necessity, or it brings you joy, or it is something you can't live without. If the answer is yes, then place it back. If not, then eliminate it. Sell, donate, toss or recycle the item.

You can use the "cut it in half" concept for any space. Try it with your dresser, or closet, or kitchen spices!

74. Turn Off the TV

Did you know that according to Nielsen, an average person spends 4 hours a **day** watching TV? That means that by the time you are 65, you will have watched **nine years** of television!

That number is amazing, but it is also sad.

Think of what you could be doing with that extra 9 years??? Or just the extra 4 hours from today??

So many people complain that there is not enough time for them to do what they want, yet very often it is the same people who plop themselves down in front of the TV each day for hours.

Instead, spend that time doing something that will give you value. Watching TV gives you nothing in return, but when you spend that time helping someone, working on a side business, playing with your family, going to the park, or just being still, you will gain so much more.

I challenge you...turn off the TV for the week and see what happens.

75. Quality Over Quantity

By now I am sure you realize that a big part of living simply is our physical environment. And, it should also be apparent to you that we don't need everything we think we do.

Consider which is better:

100 knickknacks that you have to clean every week taking up space on a huge shelf, where you can barely see one over the other, or 3 carefully selected pieces of art displayed tastefully on a single shelf?

25 mismatched plastic containers that never get used because they are warped, stained, or you are worried about leeching chemicals, or 5 glass storage containers neatly stacked in a row on your shelf?

When you need to purchase something, or you are decluttering, remember that quality is almost always better than quantity.

I have found that since I have fewer things, those things tend to be higher quality.

76. Pack Less

Ever since I traveled to Greece and had to carry my non-rolling suitcase everywhere we went over some rough terrain and steep hills, I have become an expert at packing light for travel.

And, even though my travel is often with children, we still manage to pack light. Of course, there is a stage where children need larger things such as strollers, or car seats, but those cannot be controlled.

What you can control is the amount of clothes and other miscellaneous things you bring.

When traveling, pack just a few outfits, and bring a packet of laundry detergent along if you need to. If there will be laundry facilities available, we usually bring outfits for 2-3 days, and then just do laundry. You can leave most of your toiletries at home as well if you are staying in a hotel – just use the shampoo they provide (and if you must bring the tiny shampoo home, then make sure you use it right away, instead of stashing it in the cabinet). Limit games and toys to 1-2 per child, and pick things that will keep their attention for long spans, but are easy to carry (pen and paper, activity books, etc.). Traveling with less makes it so much simpler to travel!

77. Carry On Only

Since you are packing less (see #76), then you should be able to pack everything in a carry on suitcase.

This not only saves on time to get out of the airport and through customs, etc., but also saves on fees, as more airlines are charging a per bag surcharge. And, there are also no worries about lost baggage either!

If you need your hands free while traveling, consider a nice backpack as your carry on suitcase, otherwise a simple rolling suitcase will do!

I hardly ever check luggage anymore, even when traveling with children, since their items can more than fit into their own carry on suitcase!

And a trick for fitting all your clothes...roll them! It doesn't take but a minute, but rolling your clothes allows you to pack so much more into the same space.

78. Get Out Of Debt

There are two main areas where simplification can make a huge impact in your life. The first is your physical space - your "stuff", and the second is your finances.

When you purpose to get out of debt and stay out of debt, you feel as though a huge burden has been lifted.

For many people, myself included, debt is a cause of stress and struggle. And while I am not completely debt free (yet), I have overcome several debts, and paid them off completely. I can tell you that the freedom that comes with paying off debt is amazing and it grows each time a new debt is paid!

Getting out of debt comes down to two things: reduce expenses and increase income, and live below your means. Eliminate unnecessary expenses in your budget and at the same time see what you can do to increase your income as well. Then, stay below your income level...as far below it as you can...so that you can use the extra income to pay off your debts.

I recommend paying off debts from smallest to largest, so that there is instant gratification and motivation to continue. Once one is paid, just take that extra payment and apply it to the next debt in line! It's a long process but stay the course!

79. Just Do It

Did you know that we put unnecessary stress in our lives when we procrastinate?

Whether we are procrastinating on a task that we want to do, but perhaps it seems daunting, or on a task that we have no desire to do, but know that we must do, either way, we are creating an environment of stress.

Procrastinating about something can lead to dangerous results as well. If we procrastinate long enough then a project or task becomes so urgent that it may be late or there may be consequences of us not doing it right away.

It's much better to face the giant and JUST DO IT!

On a larger project that you want to do, it's usually just a matter of getting started to build the momentum to continue, so break down the project into smaller tasks and pick one to start on.

For things that we don't want to do, we often build them up in our minds so that the tasks appears more difficult than it is in reality, so just get started! Do the first step. Then do the next step. And before you know it, you will be done!

80. Don't Participate in Negativity

I haven't watched the news in over 10 years (with one exception), and I haven't read a newspaper (except in passing) for even longer. I don't look at the top news stories on Yahoo (unless it's something that someone has told me will impact me directly).

Why?

I choose to no longer participate in negativity.

The more negativity we take in, the more stress it creates, and the worse we feel. Instead, I choose to spend my time focusing on the positive. By focusing on the positive you feel better and take things in stride.

So, turn off the news tonight. Don't read the paper anymore (better yet, save the money and the clutter and just cancel your subscription). Don't read negative stories on the Internet. Trust me, if something is big and you need to know about it, someone else will tell you.

Instead, go read a good, positive, uplifting book!

81. The 30 Day Test

Picture this: you are shopping for something specific in the mall, but you walk by a store and see this fantastic gizmo in the window that you just **have** to have. You walk in, make the purchase, and bring it home. The happiness from that purchase lasts about 2.4 hours and by that evening, you are wondering why you bought that gizmo after all.

You are not alone! It's called impulse buying and it's the reason why stores have windows and ads and they display things! They are *hoping* that you are going to buy something on impulse.

When that something is small, the impact is small (usually more clutter), but when it's larger, the impact can be larger too (interest that you have to pay on that purchase because you put it on a credit card!).

So, next time you want something that you see, write it down. Post it up on the fridge with the date and give it 30 days to mull it over. If, after the 30 days are up, it is still something that you **need**, and you have the means to get it, then feel free. Chances are, however, that most of what is on your list you will no longer feel the need to get.

82. Let Go

Probably the hardest areas of things to simplify are those things that have some sort of sentimental value.

This could be something that reminds you of someone or someplace, or an item that you received as a gift or inherited from someone special to you.

Let go. Good or bad. Let go.

Know that the person or event is not wrapped up in the item. If the item is something that when you see it, it evokes a feeling, try taking a picture of the item, and then eliminating the physical piece.

Or, perhaps your Aunt Sue gave you this vase that you absolutely think is awful, but you feel bad about getting rid of it. In this case, you could take a picture of the item in use and send it to the gift giver with a thank you note, and then get rid of it.

Let it go. Especially those items that you don't like, since those things bring bad feelings every time you see them.

83. Slow and Steady Wins the Race

If you have something to do that will take some time, don't be discouraged. Remember the story of the tortoise and hare, and take it slow and steady.

Press forward to your goal, whether it is a project that needs to be finished, or a habit you are trying to create (or break), or a room that you are decluttering.

Remember, slow and steady wins the race.

Just do something, no matter how small, each day. Break larger projects into manageable chunks and do one at a time. Break your goals into checkpoints and actions and then focus on what you can do toward that goal.

Remember, slow and steady wins the race.

84. Clear Emotional Clutter

Emotional clutter is one of the worst kinds of clutter you can have. I think emotional clutter is more devastating than physical clutter, because physical clutter is easier to clean up.

Emotional clutter is our "baggage", it's how we react to the present, based on our past experiences.

When we carry negative past experiences into the present, we are not only reliving the emotions associated with that negative experience, but also contaminating the current experience at the same time.

Find out what emotional clutter you have in your life. Do you react the same negative way each time you are in a specific situation? Did something happen in your childhood or past that you are carrying with you every day? Are you bitter at someone for hurting you? Have you withheld forgiveness out of anger?

Pray about your emotional clutter, and ask God to help you clear the past hurts and baggage away, so that you can enter into the present moment without carrying the past with you. Let go of bitterness. Forgive others. Face your fears. God will never leave you or forsake you.

85. Stop Collecting

I'm not sure what about collecting entices us so much, but most of us have had (or currently have) a collection of some sort at one point. When I was little, I collected stamps and coins, and although I have no idea what happened to the stamps, part of the coin collection ended up being stolen from me, and then I voluntarily sold the rest.

Later in life, I also collected Boyd's Bears. A relative started this collection for me, and I thought they were so cute, but looking back, I don't really see what I saw then? (Hindsight is always 20/20!) So, several years ago, I sold off most of that collection and now just have a few choice pieces left behind. And even those will be on the chopping block when I get to decluttering my guest room where they currently reside.

And at this point I do still admit to having one collection…a Pandora bracelet, that I have collected charms to represent different parts of my life. However, out of all the collections, this one has by far gotten the most use! It was, after all, one of my 33 items I used for the past 4 months, so I wore it often, and I can see adding a charm or two that were meaningful to me over the next few years.

In my experience, if your collection is not something you use daily, and perhaps you are tired of dusting it or keeping up with cleaning it,

I would just recommend you get rid of it, and just stop collecting.

86. Work in Blocks of Time

Studies show that you get more done in less time when you work in blocks of time.

I know for some, especially those with small children, working in large blocks of time is impossible! So you need to be ready to take advantage of small blocks of time, 15 minutes here and there, whenever possible. Have a list of things that you can do that don't take more than 15 minutes, so that when a 15 minute break arises, you can take full advantage of it.

If you are able to work in larger blocks of time, it's highly recommended, because your level of focus is increased when working in a block of time. In every block of time, some of the time is spent preparing to work, so the larger the block of time, the less percentage of time is spent preparing and gathering things, and the larger percentage of time is spent on actually working on the project or task at hand.

I like to make phone calls for work in blocks of time, and also larger projects get assigned blocks of time as well. And, within each block of time, I try to just focus on one task or project for the entire time.

Where in your schedule do you see a block of time, and what will you work on?

87. Delegate

When you look at your list of things to do, what do you see that can be delegated?

The rule is that if you will earn more than you will spend paying someone else to do it, then delegate it.

For example, if you paid someone to mow your lawn, and instead worked for 30 minutes, would you make more money than what it costs to pay someone to mow your lawn? If so, then it's a good investment of time and money to delegate the job of mowing your lawn.

In looking at your list, there are items that only you can do. These are things that you are really good at, your core activities. There are also things that you love to do. These things are the ones you want to focus on yourself. All else, if possible, can be delegated to someone else to do.

What can you delegate?

88. Eliminate

Here's another way to look at your list of things to do: could you eliminate some of the things on your list?

Ask yourself, "What would the consequences be if this task did not get completed?"

Then weigh the options.

Chances are you will find several things that are on your list that no longer need to be there at all, and you can eliminate them completely.

Eliminate as much as possible that is not essential for your success, or central to your mission, values and goals in life.

Focus on what matters most to you.

89. Wise Gift Giving

Most parents with children know how it feels to be inundated with gifts from well wishing family members for your children or yourself.

I love the spirit of giving, and have never discouraged gift giving from well-meaning family and friends.

But, I have been able to offer wise counsel in the area of gift giving.

Throughout the year, I will keep a list of items that either the children have wanted, or that they could use. I offer these suggestions to friends and family when it comes time for gifts, so that their gifts will be put to good use.

When toys are purchased, I suggest high quality toys that last and are educational and entertaining. Most often, they are the classic toys that have been around for a while.

I also encourage gifts that are experiences: tickets to a movie, dinner at a special place, passes to the local aquarium, or tuition for piano lessons. All of these activities provide an experience that creates a memory and, in my opinion, are far superior gifts than a toy that will be played with once or twice and then discarded.

90. Leverage Your Time

I have found that there are many daily activities that give you the opportunity to leverage your time.

When you leverage your time, you get more value than the time you put in.

For example, when I am doing the dishes, I can also be listening to a training conference call. Or, when I am grocery shopping, I can take one of my children and have them help me while spending quality one-on-one time with them talking. Or, when I am traveling in my car, I can listen to professional development audiotapes instead of the radio.

These are all examples where the value is worth more than the time.

The same is true when you invest time to accomplish things in the future. An example here would be investing an hour into creating a filing cabinet system that will save you hundreds of hours over the life of the filing cabinet (time saved finding things and filing things).

What ways can you leverage your time today?

91. Limit Mindless Activities

How many times have you hopped online to "just check your email really quickly" and then an hour later you get off, having surfed around and bounced from blog to blog.

Mindless activities like web surfing tend to suck us in! And they definitely don't help to simplify our lives. In fact, given the amount of time wasted that could have been used for other things that were more important, I would say mindless activities complicate our lives.

Be on the lookout for time sucking activities and put a stop to them immediately!

It may take a few times to realize that you have been sucked in to one of those activities yet again, but be vigilant, because your time (and your sanity) are worth it!

92. Reduce Hobbies

I love hobbies, and have a few I enjoy myself. In fact, I highly encourage everyone to have a hobby that they enjoy. The problem lies when there are too many hobbies.

Here's the thing with hobbies...most require some sort of equipment. And equipment can quickly add up in space and money spent. Times that by the number of hobbies and you have a mess.

Perhaps there are hobbies that you once participated in that no longer interest you? That's okay! Let them go. Sell your equipment and close the door on your past. When we keep hanging on to the things we are no longer interested in, we feel guilty for not doing that hobby every time we see a piece of the equipment for it. Do yourself a favor...let it go.

At any given moment, I would suggest that you have no more than three serious hobbies. Less than three is just fine too! If you have too many, then none of your hobbies get your attention. So, focus on the few that bring you great joy and remove yourself from the rest. Don't be afraid to move on or try new things if you find you are no longer interested. Feelings change over time, and that is normal! Just focus on the ones you truly love.

93. Focus on the Important

Stephen Covey has a wonderful matrix in his book *First Things First* that helps us see where our time should be spent.

Things usually fall into one of the following four categories: urgent and important, not urgent and important, urgent and not important, or not urgent and not important. The items that are urgent (whether important or not) usually get most of our time. Unfortunately, that means the items that are not urgent, but important to us often get overlooked or put on the back burner. These tasks are the ones that we should give the most attention to.

Tasks that matter most to us, those that move us deeply, are usually important, but not urgent and can be overlooked in the influx of urgent things. So, take time to refocus on what is important, especially if it is not urgent, and make a decision to spend time working toward those goals.

94. Set Boundaries

Children thrive better with boundaries. And adults can achieve greater balance with boundaries as well.

When we create a boundary, we are showing our priorities.

If you always bring work home, which interrupts family dinners, which is your priority? But instead, if you work to be more productive at work, so that you don't have to bring anything home, but can instead enjoy your family dinner, it speaks to an entirely different priority. Even if you have to bring home extra work, but choose to do it after children are in bed, and can still enjoy a nice family dinner, again this speaks to where your priorities are.

One of the best things you can do for your work and for your family is to create a boundary between work and family. When you are at work, then work hard. And when you are home, then focus on your family.

For those who work from home, like me, it's even more important to keep this boundary line in place, because it's really easy to work "just a little more" in your home office! Stop! Set a boundary, and stick to it!

95. Slow Down

It seems like everything happens at such a fast pace nowadays. People scarf down their fast food lunch while running an errand or talk on the phone while driving to work.

Instead, make a point to slow down today.

Sit down and enjoy your lunch. Eat slowly, savoring each bite.

Run an errand and focus on what you are doing.

Talk on the phone and be present for your conversation with a friend.

Drive to work and enjoy the magnificent scenery around you.

Slow down.

96. Spend Time Alone

As much as I love to spend time with others, especially my family, there is something rejuvenating about spending time alone.

When I am alone with my thoughts I reflect on the blessings I have, and thank God for them. And many times as my thoughts wander, I will find a solution for a problem I have been working on, or an idea will come to mind that is amazing! I love to be alone.

I encourage you to find time to be alone as well. Not doing something, not reading a book, just sitting quietly and taking in the world around you.

Since alone time doesn't come frequently for me at home, I usually find that driving in the car provides some quality alone time as well (just make sure to keep an eye on the road!).

Spend time alone and just be.

97. Enjoy the Silence

I love silence. I would gladly choose silence over music or noise any day.

But our world is full of noise – noise from people, cars, and sirens.

So next time you find the chance, enjoy the silence instead.

Driving alone in your car is a great place that I find silence. But I also find it on a walk, or when I get up early when the rest of the house is asleep.

Before the hustle and bustle begins again, take five minutes to enjoy the silence.

98. Forgive

When we withhold forgiveness, whom do you think is most affected? Is it you or the person who hurt you?

We are always the most affected.

When you harbor resentment, anger and bitterness toward another, those emotions wreak havoc in your life.

The person who hurt us is oblivious to our anger or bitterness, and feels no ill effects of our inability to forgive them. We, on the other hand, feel the full force of our negative emotions spiritually, mentally and physically. Yes, we truly are in more pain and agony for choosing not to forgive.

And so we have a choice. We can choose to remain bitter and angry, or we can choose to let go and forgive. Forgive the person who has wronged you whether they have asked for your forgiveness or not. Forgive them whether they deserve it or not.

Just forgive.

99. Stop Worrying

Worrying can lead to a host of problems, none of which are necessary.

When we worry, we cause our bodies to shift into high gear – the "fight or flight" response is triggered – and a host of physical symptoms and problems can appear.

Worrying accomplishes nothing but increases your stress levels considerably.

Focus on what you can control, which is your response and your level of worry.

Some, including myself, find it helpful to pray and give our problems and worries to God. Others find meditation or breathing exercises helpful to decrease levels of worry.

A little worry is okay in some situations, like worrying about how you will do on a test, but in things that you cannot control in your life, like whether or not you will get hurt, be safe, but then stop worrying.

100. Live Each Day to the Fullest

No one is guaranteed tomorrow.

So, it is up to us to live each day as if it were our last.

If you knew that today was your last day alive, what would you have done differently? Would you still have chosen to do the things you did? Or would you have changed something?

If you knew today was your last, would you choose to watch TV, or play with your child? Would you choose to argue or to forgive? Would you choose to rush through your day, or would you take time to give a hug?

Don't wait until it is too late to let those you care about know how important they are to you. Let them know you love them every day. Don't wait until it's too late to do what matters most to you. Leave a legacy for those yet to come.

Don't wait until it's too late to live each day to the fullest. Tomorrow may never come.

101. Give Back

And now we come to one of my favorites. Whenever you acquire new information that impacts you in some small way, take time to pass it along to someone else.

Pay it forward so that others can learn from you.

If you have experienced something, share it so others may learn from your failures and your successes.

This book is my way of giving back a little. Throughout the years I have learned these lessons, have experienced putting these strategies for simple living into play in my own life. And I have reaped great rewards.

I now pass this knowledge to you, in hopes that you will pass it along to someone else.

Give back. Give back to others. Give back to your community. Give back to the world.

You can and do make a difference.

Thank You!

Thank you for reading this book! I hope and pray that it has been a blessing to you.

I wish you the best on your journey to simplification!

You can connect with me on my blog: www.ThisMessyHome.com

Made in the USA
Lexington, KY
28 July 2014